Your Next Big Idea!

A 4-Step Process for

Evaluating the Potential

of Your Next Business Project

By

Sammy Teather
(Ba Hons, ACIM DipM, QTS)

Kim Morrison
(FCMI, DipMgmt)

www.teatherandmorrisononline.com
Copyright 2016

This Book is for You if You...

- Own or manage a small or medium sized business
- Are an entrepreneur
- Are considering starting a small business
- Are a service provider
- Are selling physical products
- Are an online seller

It is also for you if you...

- Want a simple repeatable process for evaluating a potential project idea before sinking money and time into it
- Want to find a profitable niche in your marketplace
- Want to learn how to focus on the opportunities that have the highest chance of succeeding
- Want to be able to tell if a potential BIG idea is, frankly, a 'no go' area!

Hello from Sammy and Kim

None of the information in this book contains complicated maths, or long passages of theory to remember and you won't be asked to sign up for anything or buy any 'extras'.

In fact, because we have spent the time studying, working and refining this methodology over the years, everything you need is included right here, even handy worksheets to help you get your ideas and thoughts on paper!

This guide describes techniques that help you analyse your projects or services and covers the factors to make better decisions about which projects to develop and which to leave well alone.

However, success in business is not an exact science and you will still need to think rationally, apply due diligence and make some judgment calls.

Unfortunately, no tool exists that can tell you with 100% certainty whether a new project will work or not. In fact, if anyone ever approaches you with a 'sure thing for 100% success' you should be very sceptical indeed.

Like everything else, success in business is based on planning and hard work, but this book will walk you through the exact steps you need to take. It will also equip you with the skills you need to be able to make an informed decision.

We have created several Activity sheets and forms for you to record your progress as you work through your ideas, as well as checklists to monitor your progress.

Downloadable copies of these are all available online at:

www.teatherandmorrisononline.com/nextbigideachecklists

We did also work through our own process in developing this book and would particularly like to thank Albert Peters of Pegasus HR for his incredibly valuable feedback and help.

Contents

Introduction

Wouldn't it be wonderful to know the chances of success for a new project, product, or service BEFORE you start spending money?

Too often business owners create products and services based on little more than a gut feeling, and then throw every selling technique conceivable at them in the hope they will sell... but this is the EXACT OPPOSITE of the approach you should be following when developing new products and services.

You should determine the need first, then build your offer around that need.

Basically, it's much easier to sell something when your product or service is in high demand!

During this course in a book you will learn the exact steps to follow for determining if your product or service idea is worth pursuing. As is? ...with a few tweaks? ...or not at all?

You will also learn how to use tools available online and how to analyse the results you get from them.

However tempting it is to fall in love with a new idea, you need to always remember that you are in business to make a profit.

Why Aren't More Companies Doing This?

The simple answer is that many businesses operating today are small businesses who have no formal training in the evaluation and comparison of projects.

Large corporations use finance experts with advanced degrees to perform complex calculations and report the results to management.

When department managers receive the results, they are responsible for interpreting them, yet many do not possess the skills required to understand the analysis provided.

This can explain why often projects in government and corporations do not succeed.

By the time you finish this book, you'll be able to:

- ➤ Evaluate your new project, product, or service ideas quickly, and for no more than the cost of this book
- ➤ Use our proven 4-step process so you can determine whether to invest additional time and resources implementing your new idea
- ➤ Assess the potential for earning income from your proposed project, so that you can gauge whether it is a viable business idea
- ➤ Identify the needs and challenges of your market in relation to what you have to offer
- ➤ Estimate the potential customer demand for your idea

➢ Answer essential questions about the possible longevity of your product or service
➢ Decide whether your idea will be able to grow over time
➢ Determine the unique qualities your product or service can provide
➢ Evaluate it against what your competitors have to offer.

You will then be able to see whether there's an opportunity to carve out your own niche market or edge out the competition.

As you've probably guessed, you'll be doing a lot of evaluation and asking some difficult questions. However, these are essential steps to take before investing a lot of time and money into something new.

It really is best to do the groundwork now and assess it to see if you can succeed at your new venture before you start the process of implementing it!

Activity 1

Make a list of potential projects you are thinking of pursuing. It makes no difference if they are products or services.

SO WHAT'S YOUR NEXT BIG IDEA?		
Project Idea	Type	Notes
Identify ONE project from your list to evaluate first:		

Keep your list handy in case the first product you choose doesn't pass the tests.

STEP 1

Evaluate the Market Profitability Potential

In this first step, you will learn about two types of market research methods and learn how to make a judgement about which is the best one to use for evaluating the market for your idea.

You will also learn how to use some advanced search operators in Google to determine the profitability potential of your market. Search operators are words that can be added to searches to help narrow down the results.

How to Gauge the Size of the Market

In order to gauge the size of your market, you will need to perform some market research.

There are two types of research: Primary and Secondary.

Primary Research

- Primary research interacts directly with potential customers. It is in the form of surveys, questionnaires, contests, etc.
- The goal is to find interest in your product or service.

Secondary Research

- Secondary research comes from gathered data.
- This data is gathered internally or externally from industry and government sources.

TOP TIP:

A note on surveys: surveys report intention and intention does not always translate to sales.

For that reason, you should cut the number of people who responded positively in half to account for this statistical variance.

How to Conduct Primary Research

Primary research is research where you ask questions and gather data yourself.

What makes it primary is that you are the one who did the research and uncovered it for your specific purposes.

Primary research may include questionnaires, interviews, surveys, or focus groups where you go straight to your existing and/or potential customers for their feedback.

1. Ask customers what they think

...AND listen to their answers.

Ask customers and potential customers what they think about your product or service:

- Would they buy it?
- How often would they buy it?
- How much would they pay for it?
- What do they use that serves this need at the moment?
- Who do they currently buy it from?
- Why would / why wouldn't they consider switching?

A note on asking friends and family...

- While you can ask friends and family for their input be aware that they might just telling you what they think you want to hear.
- It is ALWAYS better to ask people who are actually in your target market, even if it is not so convenient.

2. Talk to similar businesses

If you think that no one in your field would share this stuff, you may be mistaken.

Networking groups, such as the Chamber of Commerce, are set up specifically for this and, in our experience, are quite helpful in giving a new business some direction.

Posing as a potential customer and visiting successful businesses that are similar to yours is also a great way of gaining really useful information.

3. Conduct a survey of people in your target market

Conducting a survey of people in your market, either at a relevant offline location or online, can give you useful feedback.

'Relevant' means a place relevant to your business, such as a sports club if your business sells sporting goods.

Remember it is good practice to ask for permission from the manager or owner before doing this if you don't own the location!

If you are hoping to sell a service, include questions about the importance customers attach to it and not just the features they want most. Previous customers' testimonials and reviews can be valuable and also find out whether you need to be a member of a certain trade or professional body.

4. Contact industry organisations

Contact organisations and official bodies in your industry and speak to their representatives.

You will be amazed at how much useful information is available, including forecasts of upcoming trends and news of new market opportunities and grants.

Remember to think outside the box – if you are providing a specialist service, why not include industries who may not have expertise in your specialist area but might be interested in using you to streamline their business. For example, a medium sized food manufacturing firm would possibly be interested in a logistics specialist with knowledge of refrigeration **and** food health and safety accreditation.

5. Ask the right questions

This sounds obvious, but make sure you are asking questions that will help you make your decision.

It's easy to start asking questions that are irrelevant to the main issue which right now is "IS THIS MARKET GOING TO BE PROFITABLE FOR ME OR NOT?"

Do not fall into the trap of actively promoting your product or service at this time - you just need unbiased feedback for now.

Are you coaching your respondents to give the answers you want by the way you ask the question?
e.g. *"Would you prefer to eat greasy fast food from a chain or a*

lovely, freshly made roast dinner from a friendly local gastro-pub?"

Some questions require just a 'Yes' or 'No' answer. These are quick to ask and quick to analyse but will they give you the quality of information you need?

Giving your respondent a chance to elaborate on their answer will take longer to evaluate. It will give you a far greater insight though into those crucial 'Who? Where? When? Why? How? How Often? How Many? And How Much would you be prepared to Pay?' questions that need answers before you start your new venture.

6. A 'Yes I would be interested...' is **NOT** a definite sale

Please, please, please do not make the assumption that a positive response on a questionnaire is a future customer.

What you are gathering is a general 'feel' for the size of the market and when a potential customer says they would be interested in your new product or service THIS DOES NOT MEAN they would definitely buy it, OR that if they did they would buy it from YOU. (Sorry☹)

It is worth saying again that you should halve the number of positive responses to gain an indication of actual intent.

How to Conduct Secondary Research

Secondary research is research that has already been gathered for another purpose by someone else. It is where you analyse data that has already been published.

There are many ways to conduct secondary research using the wealth of information online – some is free, but these days most require payment.

1. Keyword research

Keyword research is an important, valuable, and high return activity as it is a great way to look at search volume and demographics for certain keywords related to your product or service idea.

It will also be useful later when you develop your website as ranking for the right keywords will help you get found more easily online.

By researching your market's keyword demand at this stage, you will learn more about your customers as a whole. It will also help you identify the right type of customers for your idea.

This type of intelligence is really useful as it will help you produce the products and services that web searchers are actively seeking.

2. Competitor research

Includes looking at their premises, websites and social media.

See if there is a forum or questions relating to your product or service, or to one similar to your idea, that will give you useful information about what your competitors' customers like and dislike about their offering.

This is very useful research as it shows you where you can improve and offer a better service when you launch your version.

3. Blogs and websites

Read blogs and browse websites to better understand your market or industry.

If you are selling a physical product, see if it is sold on Amazon, and, if so, read the reviews.

If you are a tradesman, read reviews on TrustATrader, Checkatrade or Trusted Trader. For a hotel, restaurant or B&B, you could do the same on Trip Advisor.

4. Join social media groups

Join social media groups and listen in on conversations among your target market.

Facebook has groups covering almost any area you can think of.

If there isn't a group on Facebook, you can do some primary research and start your own group to see what feedback/interest you get.

5. Contact industry organisations

These often have readily available data and information dedicated to industry trends and improvement.

It is quite often free or heavily discounted if you fulfil certain criteria, for instance being a member of a related trade body or union, so do ask if you qualify before paying out.

Which Market Research Method is Best?

Ideally you should use both primary and secondary research methods to get the most useful data about your chosen product or service.

The order you do this in is really up to you.

Old school thinking says to gather the secondary data first but, in our opinion, particularly for niche and locally based markets, some secondary data can be too general.

For instance, a small local flower shop specialising in Wedding Bouquets needs very different data from a supermarket chain selling bunches of flowers in the foyer of every branch in the UK.

However, secondary data is undoubtedly an invaluable guide to upcoming industry trends and a useful indicator of market saturation.

Primary research is more labour-intensive for you but it yields direct feedback that's very useful, as long as people are being truthful and your questions are unbiased.

It is also worth remembering that people want to please and will sometimes say what they think you want to hear rather than risk offending you.

How to Start Your Market Potential Evaluation

Once you have conducted your market research, you will need to begin to assess the size of your potential market place.

No amount of research will give you an exact number about your market size so you will need to make decisions using the research you have conducted as guidance.

Activity 2

Start by conducting a simple search for your product or service on Google. If you are planning to sell in the UK only, you may want to search exclusively for UK sites.

If your product or service has not been developed yet, try to find products and services that offer similar features.

If you can't find any, then use keywords from the industry itself.

As an example, suppose the product you are considering is a cat toy.

If a specific product name does not exist, use the category, i.e., cat toys.

Start with a search in Google with that phrase, which has close to 6.5 million results (March 2016 figures). Obviously, this is a popular market. This is good.

Now refine your search to narrow the focus to what you are proposing to sell, for instance, "interactive cat toys for kittens".

The results are significantly less.

Drill down using a variety of keywords and phrases until you have an idea of the size of interest in your specific market niche.

You should always look at the variations on a phrase and account for them when sizing up your market potential.

Further Refinement

The searches outlined so far are called broad match searches.

This means that Google may include results that contain the word "cat", or the word "toys" or even the words "interactive" and "kittens" for the second example.

While Google has become better at making searches more relevant for the entire keyword phrase, the results you are getting may not show you the true picture.

You now need to narrow down the search to websites that are optimising for your key search term.

To do that, you can use an advanced operator within Google.

Having the keyword phrase as part of the title will help Google determine what the web page is about.

You can use the '**allintitle:**' search operator to return only those results with that specific phrase in the title, as follows:

allintitle:interactive cat toys for kittens

When you search using operators or punctuation marks, don't add any spaces between the operator and your search terms or it won't work.

Now, we have said that this is not an exact science, and even these results can become skewed as you look past the first few pages.

However, the results ARE going to be close to the number of websites that are in competition for that keyword phrase, and this is going to be good enough to give you a pretty close idea of what is going on with your idea.

Ideas for Service providers:

Again, Google is a great place to start your search for competitors and a good way to attract service providers is to pose as a potential customer wanting a specific service (your next BIG idea) in a specific location (the one you are targeting).

LinkedIn is a good place to target for this type of information as service providers will always be on the lookout for potential customers.

We would recommend setting up a new free email address with a fake pseudonym which does not contain any personal or business identification, such as bob.m.j.smithson@yahoo.com *(apologies if you are Bob and this is your email address – but congratulations, you are now in a book!)*

You are suddenly going to be getting a lot of emails from your competitors fishing for your business, which you can read, learn from and reply to with searching questions if you want more information.

When you receive these emails, try to remain flexible and open minded – if a competitor says there is no call for your service, they may just mean they do not do it…OR they may have found there is no call for it, OR that something else works better. Get chatty and ask them why they don't do it and why they are recommending something different… you may be glad you did!

Activity 3

Number of Competitors

In the first section of Step 1, you were shown how to find competitors for your next BIG idea.

This also gives you some indication of who in your market is actively competing for a percentage share of the marketplace.

Make a list of these competitors here:

Competitor	Website URL
	www.
	www.
	www.
	www.
	www.
	www.
	www.
	www.
	www.
	www.

Once you have a list of competitors from that search, you can use them to find others.

Google has a '**related:**' search operator.

This search works with the URLs (www.'s) you have now listed.

Sometimes you won't get any results for a website that you enter using the **'related:'** operator function.

If the first 'www.' you use does not return any results, simply try another on your list.

This is often because larger companies sell a wide range of products and so may be using wider, more generic categories, for instance 'Cat Accessories' or 'Secretarial Services'.

Try to target websites that are more closely related to selling your niche product, in this example, cat toys, or better yet, interactive cat toys. In a service industry it could be, Legal Secretarial Services.

Of course, you would have to alter this to whatever product or service you are hoping to target.

Spending time narrowing down your search will give a more accurate indication of the number of competitors you actually have.

Look out for Companies who are Advertising

Advertising is expensive, so it is usually done by:

- Successful companies who are selling lots and want to sell more

Or

- New start-ups who need to advertise to 'get the ball rolling'

Businesses shouldn't be spending money on advertising unless it is working for them.

If something is not working, for instance the cost of running the advertisement is costing more than they anticipated versus the amount of profit per sale they are making from it, they should quickly stop that campaign.

You can use this information to determine if your product or service has potential by checking whether there is currently any advertising for your product, service, or industry and how long they have been advertising for.

However, re-read the second bullet point above.

Do check the advertisers you choose to follow are not just newbies in the market who are throwing all they have at advertising campaigns in the hope of generating initial sales.

Instead look for companies with proven track records - this means they should know what they are doing.

Follow the ads you choose as relevant over a certain time period and see how they develop.

If your competitors have a social media presence, follow them on all the platforms they use.

A quick note on social media platforms

Make sure you sign up for notifications and when your competitor posts something make a point of 'liking' it. This will indicate to the social media provider's algorithm (e.g., Facebook or Twitter) that you like what they are sending so they will send you more of the same.

If you don't interact the algorithm will stop sending you those posts as it will think you are not interested.

TOP TIP

When you search in Google, the top of the results will usually contain ads.

Search using product-related keywords and take a screen shot of your results (**ctrl > prt sc** on your PC keyboard) and save it in a new document in Word, PowerPoint, or Excel.

Do this daily for a week or more.

Look for advertisers that continue running the same ads.

Try to avoid the temptation to keep clicking on competitors ads as it will skew the results the competitor is getting from actual potential customers and will give you a false reading.

Remember your mission is to gather REAL TARGET MARKET INFORMATION, not to nobble the competition!

If companies are consistently advertising a product or service, it's a good indication they are making money from it.

You can go through the same exercise with the following:

- Manta.com
- YP.com
- Ads from Social Media
- Magazines – check your library to find back issues.

There are also several tools available that show what kinds of advertising your competitors are using.

Examples of these include Google Alerts and Social Mention.

Why Competition Can Be Good for Your Business

- Competition indicates a viable market for a product or service.
- It keeps all players on top of their game and weeds out those who become complacent.
- Innovation stays strong in competitive markets.
- Competition can help lower the cost of manufacturing products and services.
- It can lead companies to invent lower-cost manufacturing processes, which can increase their profits, help them compete and pass those savings on to the consumer.
- You can learn from your competition in several ways.
- When your potential competition is successful, you'll be able to see what works and use the same techniques for your own success.

- It's good to see failures too because you won't have to waste your time and resources doing something that clearly doesn't work.
- It's valuable information to have and use.
- Your competition helps you define your business within your marketplace. By becoming familiar with what they are doing on a daily basis, you can inform the decisions you are going to have to make in deciding whether to pursue your BIG idea.
- This information helps you discern how you will need to compete in the niche you've chosen and prepares you for the task to come.

To find out more about your competitors, try the following:

Sign up to your competitors newsletters

- Go through your list of competitors and see which of them offer newsletters.
- Sign up to those newsletters.
- This is a great way to keep track of them and get notifications of any updates and promotions.

Use your pseudonym email to do this as before and they will quite happily send you lots of advertising automatically!

Use Google Alerts

- Set up Google Alerts (alerts.google.com) and use the name of your competitors as the keywords.
- Whenever something new appears in Google about those competitors, you will get an alert.

'Follow' them on Social Media

- Respond when you see their posts with a 'like' so the algorithm knows you are interacting or the feed will stop.

Buy products and services from your competitors

If you have the budget, pose as a customer and buy your competitors' products and/or services that are similar to the ones you are hoping to sell.

Pay attention to the sales process and how you are treated.

Contact customer service and ask questions.

Make note of any strengths and weaknesses in their business processes.

Look at the FAQs, Frequently Asked Questions, on their website if they have them.

If you sell physical products, check out Amazon, eBay, Not On The Highstreet, etc.

Your competitors may be selling on these platforms.

With Amazon, you can see how well a product is selling via its product rank (the best-selling items are on page one) and eBay will show you completed listings of products, whether they sold and for how much.

Activity 4

A strengths, weaknesses, opportunities and threats (S.W.O.T) diagram is a really useful way of analysing how your competitors sit within your marketplace, and how much of a threat they are to your business.

Use the S.W.O.T. diagrams below to list the competitors you highlighted in Activity 2 and note their strengths and weaknesses in the top two boxes. Then make a note of any opportunities you can see to capitalise on their weaknesses. Also make a note of any threats you can see that you will have to find a way to compete with.

Take time to really think about each competitor and what they offer their customers.

Think about how their customers see their product, its good points and things that could be improved. Think about their service, their location, their staffing, opening hours and branding...in fact think about anything and everything that could be giving them the edge, OR is an opportunity for you to make your mark.

Competitor 1	
Strengths	Weaknesses
Opportunities	Threats

Competitor 2	
Strengths	Weaknesses
Opportunities	Threats

Competitor 3

Strengths	Weaknesses
Opportunities	Threats

Competitor 4

Strengths	Weaknesses
Opportunities	Threats

Competitor 5

Strengths	Weaknesses
Opportunities	Threats

Competitor 6

Strengths	Weaknesses
Opportunities	Threats

Competitor 7	
Strengths	Weaknesses
Opportunities	Threats

Competitor 8	
Strengths	Weaknesses
Opportunities	Threats

Competitor 9

Strengths	Weaknesses
Opportunities	Threats

Competitor 10

Strengths	Weaknesses
Opportunities	Threats

Considerations for Digital Products

If you're planning to sell some type of digital product, there are a number of online marketplaces where you will be able to list your product.

These sites also provide a wealth of information you can tap into for assessing the potential of your current BIG idea.

ClickBank and Amazon

ClickBank and Amazon are two of the most popular marketplaces for both digital AND physical products.

You can use them to gather information on products similar to yours, as outlined in the previous pages.

If possible, buy the products and test them yourself.

Read through the reviews, both good and bad.

Use the good reviews as a clue to the types of topics people enjoyed and use the bad reviews to improve your product or service.

Take notes of the strengths, weaknesses, opportunities and threats they pose to you and your BIG idea.

In many digital marketplaces, you can also see the statistics for what is selling well and what isn't.

While part of poor performance can be due to a simple lack of marketing, look for trends in specific types of products and work out where the revenue stream is coming from.

With digital products the revenue is often coming from the 'added extras' or in-app purchases.

Lastly, always ask yourself if you and your new digital product will be able to 'take on' the big players in that niche?

It is not always about having a better product... unfortunately, in a super competitive market, having a big backer like Disney can sell a so-so game in the millions while the better game flops.

Activity 5

1. Using the project, product, or service idea you identified in the Introduction, and taking into account all the information you have now gathered, rate your top competitors on a scale of 1 to 5, with 5 being big competition, in terms of how they match your product or service BIG idea.

	Competitor	Rating	Notes
1			
2			
3			
4			
5			
6			
7			
8			
9			
10			

2.   Over a period of time (1 week or more), take note of the sponsored advertisements on Google that appear when you search using keywords related to your product. Also review any marketing material that arrives by email and post. Remember consistent advertising of similar products or services over a sustained period suggests profitability.

3.   Note the prevalence of large companies like Amazon, Direct Line, Domino's and big supermarket chains when searching for keywords and ads. Is this a market you feel you can compete with?

Decision Time

If you find yourself up against strong competition like this, it does signify that there is a high demand, however, it might be wise to reassess your focus so you are not competing directly on elements such as price.

Brainstorm ways to narrow your product or service focus.

> **Decide whether to move forward to the next step with your proposed idea.**
>
> **If not, pick a new one from your ideas in the first activity and go through the assessment process again.**

STEP 2

Determining
Consumer Demand

However much competition there is, it makes little sense to develop a product or service if there are very few actual customers who need, want and are willing to pay for it.

In Step 2 you will learn how to determine who your potential customers are and whether there is enough of a market available for you to move forward with your big idea.

Use Surveys, Polls, and Contests to Determine What People Want

Surveys and polls are great ways to find out what kinds of products and services people are looking to buy.

You are seeking to obtain as many positive responses as possible.

As mentioned in the first step, you should then cut the number of positive responses by about half to get a better feel for who would really be interested.

Not everyone who indicates they would buy will actually do so.

Contests are a fun way to engage potential customers as people love to win prizes.

The prize offered needs to be worth the effort.

Avoid offering your new product or service as a prize because you may choose not to move forward with it after evaluation.

You should never offer something that you cannot deliver.

That can get you in to legal trouble.

If you can't think of something to offer, consider a gift card.

Facebook is a great platform for contests but do make sure you are following their competition guidelines.

Unfortunately, because Facebook changes these rules ever so often, writing the current rules here seems unwise, so we suggest you go to www.facebook.com and type 'contest guidelines' into the search bar for their latest update.

Seek Out Forums, Groups and Blogs Related to Your Niche

People love to chat about their great new finds and their purchase woes on forums and in Facebook groups.

They ask questions with the hope of finding possible solutions to their problems.

You need to find forums that are related to your product, service, or industry, which you can do by appending the word "forum" or "blog" onto your search for your product or service.

The most useful thing you can do for your BIG idea right now is just listen and learn

Don't try to influence the discussion.

Avoid pitching your product or idea.

People use forums to connect with others in a friendly manner.

It's a community and members get to know and trust each other over time.

Becoming influential on these forums can be done by helping others and developing trust.

It is much easier to sell to people from a position of trust than through cold pitches as an unknown person.

After becoming an authority figure, you can recommend your product or service when the time is right but only do this if the product or service is truly relevant to the discussions.

Determine Market Segments and Target Markets

If you use surveys, remember it is really useful to gather information about participants' age and gender.

This will give you an immediate segmenting of your market.

If you believe that people won't want to answer these more personal questions, you can use age brackets, like 20-24, etc. and (if you are gathering the data in person) make a note of the participant's gender on the form after the survey is complete.

Another trick is to view your competitors' websites, brochures, and marketing material.

- Focus on those that have pictures of people.
- What do those people look like?
- How old do they seem?
- Are they male or female?

And so on.

Find competitors who have media kits on their websites.

- Analyse the material included
- Which media are they aimed at?
- What is the target market for that media type?

Activity 6

Find Keywords to Target

Use Google's Keyword Planner to determine if your product or service has any search volume.

Keyword Planner is part of Google's AdWords program.

You will need to sign up for an account, but you won't have to pay to use the tool.

Choose keywords to enter into the Planner that would describe your product or service.

It will return suggestions for other keywords.

Observe the Average Monthly Search Volume as this will indicate interest.

Volumes over 1000 are good.

You can also see how much Google believes advertisers should pay in the Suggested Bid column - the higher the bid, the greater the competition for that keyword.

Try to find 'buyer keywords'

These may appear within the suggested keywords but you can use some qualifiers within your keyword phrases to find them.

The most obvious qualifier is the word "buy".

Product names, service names, and model numbers are also good buyer keywords.

People use them when they're ready to buy.

At that point, they are looking for pricing and vendors.

Use Amazon's instant search facility

If you are going to be selling a physical product, use Amazon's search bar to see if your potential product comes up in the dropdown list. If it does, which page is it on and how near to the top?

If you type in, for example, 'Cat toy' you will get a list of keyword suggestions pop up including: Cat Toy for Indoor Cats, Cat Toy Interactive, Cat Toy Kitten, Cat Toy Mouse, Cat Toy Laser.... these are all long tail keywords (Yes, we know these are actually phrases, but trust us, it works!)

You get the idea!

Unlike Google, people go to Amazon specifically to buy products.

If your product (or a similar one) appears as part of the instant search, this is a good indication that people want your product.

Popular Keyword Research Tools:

Here is a list of popular keyword research tools which, at the time of writing, are all free to use, but these things do change so please do check if you decide to use them.

They are also mainly USA based, so please do bear in mind the variations in spelling, word use and, of course, number of 'hits' shown. The US marketplace is much bigger than the UK marketplace so please don't be misled by the 'hits' figures.

However, in a bid to find keywords, these search engines will help you build your list of possibilities considerably.

1. **Wordtracker:** generates keywords for search engine and website optimisation.
   http://www.wordtracker.com/

2. **Keyword Discovery:** compiles keyword search stats from worldwide search engines.
   http://www.keyworddiscovery.com/

3. **Goodkeywords:** downloadable freeware that queries a number of popular search engines to identify good keywords.
   http://www.goodkeywords.com/

4. **Google Alerts:** email updates of the latest relevant Google results based on your choice of topic or keywords.
   http://www.google.com/alerts

5. **Google Suggest:** as you type in a keyword, Google offers suggestions and shows the number of results.
   http://www.google.com/webhp?hl=en&complete=1

TOP TIP:

You may be tempted to target only the most popular keywords in your niche market if you are thinking of advertising online. However, remember that these keywords have the most competition within the search engines -- meaning, you may well be fighting against hundreds (or even thousands) of competitors to get the attention of your market.

Once identified, your keywords do not HAVE to be just used online – they work everywhere!

Try using them in Email headers, Newsletters, Print advertisements, Flyers and Posters.

Keep a note of which keywords you use and where, and over time you will find you can narrow down to the few that are consistently resulting in sales.

If you do decide to advertise online, a better strategy is to focus on the middle to lower "tail" of the market by looking at the 25th-100th most popular keywords or phrases from your keyword research. Use these as the basis for your research. The competition will be much less and you can narrow down your focus to attract only those who are an ideal match for your product or service.

This will cost you less in both money and time spent talking / emailing potential customers who are not a complete match for what you want to offer.

Another thing to do, if you are a locally based product or service provider, is to put your catchment area, e.g. your county, or town, into your long tail keywords as, although this will result in less 'hits', you will achieve a much better conversion rate.

There is no point in you spending money targeting the whole of the UK if you have a locally based service.

Remember that it is not the amount of 'hits' or 'likes' a keyword generates that matters – the conversion rate is the metric you should focus on.

Product:

Long Tail Key Words	Page	Rank on page
E.g. Cat Toy for Indoor Cats Or Legal Secretarial Services	2	4
1		
2		
3		
4		
5		
6		
7		
8		
9		
10		
11		
12		

How to Create an Ideal Customer Profile

One of the things that Kim and I encounter most often is that business owners want to try to appeal to everyone.

However, one of the key rules of marketing is that you can't appeal to everyone all of the time – Niche is always preferable, whether you are a supermarket, a car dealer, a hairdresser, a coffee shop or an online entrepreneur.

You need to decide exactly WHAT you will be selling and then decide WHO you will be targeting – in that order!

Sell to people who fit within your best customer profiles.

You will actually reach fewer people by doing this, but those people will have a much higher likelihood of buying from you. This means you spend much less per customer on making those sales.

The research techniques you explored in Step 1 will have given you a good indication that people are looking for your product or service or you wouldn't have continued this far. However, knowing there is a demand doesn't tell you what types of people want your product or service or who they are.

Needs vs. Wants

Contrary to belief, it's actually a lot easier to sell something your target market WANTS as opposed to something they NEED.

If you are a Dentist, your potential customer may NEED to visit you, but it's seen as a chore, costly and easy to put off until another day. However if you target their WANT to become more attractive with a brilliantly white smile, they will make the time to book the appointment and pay for the treatment.

If you are a Business Coach, your potential customer may NEED to become more productive, worry less and sleep more, but what they WANT is to have their business streamlined so they can enjoy the benefits of being self-employed.

If you sell greetings cards, your potential customer may NEED to send a card for a friend's birthday, but they WANT is to send something they know will make the friend smile and feel loved.

Changing your focus to what a customer WANTS can make a huge difference to your strategy and to your income.

Your Product or Service:

Phrased as a NEED	=	Phrased as a WANT
Need to stop worrying	=	Want to feel on top of things
Need a cup of coffee	=	Want to sit down for 15 mins
	=	
	=	
	=	
	=	
	=	
	=	
	=	
	=	
	=	
	=	
	=	

Tracking down your ideal customer

Find websites and groups that are closely related to the product or service you are considering offering.

You can search your product or service name in Google and use the top results.

To get even more focused with your targeting, use Facebook's advertising platform to do research.

It will give you a good demographic breakdown.

You will need to sign up to Facebook's Adverts Manager but you won't have to go as far as funding the account or running an ad if you don't want to.

After signing up, click on the Create Ad link. You will be asked to choose an objective from a list.

Choose "Send people to your website" then enter a top competitor's website.

Scroll down to the 'Audience' section and set it for the UK, and then go to the 'Budget and Duration' options. Set them for 1 week and £7 (that's £1 per day).

Don't worry, you won't have to spend any money – we are setting the site up this way so that your results are comparable every time you make a search.

As you make changes using the options, Facebook updates the target audience numbers and this will give you an idea of how many people are in your target market.

Use the Detailed Targeting section and enter keywords that are related to your product or service.

If it only returns a few hundred people, that may be a sign that you either have narrowed your niche too far or that it is not a viable one.

Spend time going through as many different audiences and keywords as you can think of, and keep a note of the numbers they generate.

Even little changes, like having the same words in a different order, can actually give different results.

Words Tried	Reach

Activity 7

1. Using the template on the next page, plan a survey you can give to potential customers.

2. Ask about the demographics of your target market, as well as asking about the specific wants and needs they have.

3. What challenges do they have at the moment that they are finding difficult to get solutions for?

4. If you already have an existing email list that would be interested, send them the survey to complete.

   Even if you can't do a survey, look for competitor websites that can give you an idea of market demographics and segments.

   Include media kits and press packs in your search.

   Then note your findings!

5. Look for at least one forum and one blog related to your idea.

6. Spend time every day reading what people are saying and noting their comments.

7. Where appropriate, ask a question related to a problem your product or service would solve.

8. Take notes on what you learn about your market's wants and challenges.

What you need to find out in your Survey
About them & their location, etc.:

About their Wants and Needs:

About their present Challenges:

Other useful questions may be...

What do they use / buy at the moment to fulfil this?

How often do they buy it?

Are they happy with what they currently buy?

Where do they currently buy from?

Would they consider swapping?

Are they the buying decision maker?

Can you get in contact with them again?

Create an Ideal Customer Profile

Based on the information you've gathered so far.

Draft Ideal Customer Profile
Who are they?
Age:
Gender:
Income:
Location:
Occupation:
Education:
Family:
Other:
What specifically are his or her challenges?
1.
2.
3.
4.
5.
6.
What specifically are his or her wants and needs?
1.
2.
3.
4.
5.
6.
What specifically do they buy/use at the moment to fulfil this?

Once you have created your ideal customer profile, test it out by tracking down between 8 and 10 new people who fit this profile exactly and ask them to do your survey.

Note their answers and, if needed, adjust the ideal customer profile as necessary.

Decide whether to move forward to the next step with your proposed idea.

If not, pick a new one from your ideas in the first activity and go through the assessment process again.

STEP 3

Assess the

Long-term Potential

If your product or service is not evergreen, you will constantly be developing new products and services as the old ones go out of fashion.

This next step will help you determine if your product or service has long-term potential.

Is Your New Product or Service Evergreen?

Which would you rather do? Spend your time constantly creating new products and services or reap the benefits from products and services that will continue to sell well into the future with very little maintenance?

It takes a fair amount of money and effort to create products and services, so we are almost sure you will choose the second option, i.e., reap the benefits from products and services that will sell well into the future...

Evergreen products and services are those that will continue their opportunity for sales for many years to come. Consider the toilet bowl which has existed in its present form for decades.

There have been some minor improvements made over the years but it is fundamentally the same product as when it first started out.

Contrast this to the VCR.

Some people reading this won't even know what that was. (It was a popular device for recording TV programmes onto video tape several years ago).

Products and services that are evergreen tend to fall within the health, wealth, finance, and food categories. Technology, fashion and fad products, on the other hand, tend to become obsolete relatively quickly and are not considered evergreen.

To determine if your product or service will be evergreen, just ask yourself whether people will still want to buy it five or so years from now?

Can you foresee any new technologies or trends that might make your product or service obsolete within a few years?

Have you heard any rumours of legislation, privatisation, trade agreements or certification that might impact on your idea?

If you can think of any, list them here...

Things that may be on the horizon:

Another interesting exercise is to ask yourself what is the PURPOSE of your product or service rather than what it is.

For instance the PURPOSE of a drill is to make holes.

A laser can do this - is it a threat?
Why is your idea better?

A hole punch can do this - is it a threat?
Why is your idea better?

A nail can do this - is it a threat?
Why is your idea better?

Think of as many alternatives to the PURPOSE of your BIG idea as you can.

Be specific about the **PURPOSE** of your BIG idea.

For instance, consider the **PURPOSE** of a mobile hairdresser.

It is not actually the cutting and styling of the hair that is the purpose here.

The PURPOSE of a mobile hairdresser is to:

- Make customers feel pampered and relaxed by cutting, colouring and styling their hair in the comfort of their own homes.
- Offer home visits and hours to suit their customers. Salons and barbers work office hours and don't do house calls.
- Provide a professional service at the customer's home. A box of hair dye can be bought cheaply but is not as controllable as having it done professionally.
- Allow people who are house bound to access this service.
- Enable families to all get their hair cut in one go - especially good if there are small children involved.

Activity 8

Your New Product or Service:	
What is its Purpose?	
What else can provide this?	**Is this a future threat?**

1. List 3 features of your product or service that you believe will still be relevant in 5 years' time.

Features of my Product or Service that will still be relevant in 5 years' time
1.
2.
3.

2. List 3 features that you believe may not be relevant in 5 years' time and note improvements you can make to change that.

Features of my Product or Service that may NOT be relevant in 5 years' time
1.   *Something I could do this to change this is....*
2.   *Something I could do this to change this is....*
3.   *Something I could do this to change this is....*

3. Now note additional products or services that you consider good cross-selling opportunities to sell alongside your BIG Idea.

- Consider manuals, cases, accessories, warranties, shine protector, helpline, etc.
- Think about what other companies in your niche do.
- Think about things they DON'T do!
- Think about what will be of most benefit to your potential customer.

Additional Product / Service	Opportunity
1.	
2.	
3.	
4.	
5.	
6.	
7.	
8.	
9.	
10.	

Cross-Selling Pros and Cons...

If you have purchased a phone recently, the salesperson is likely to have tried to sell you a plan from a particular network.

Or perhaps they tried to convince you to purchase insurance on the phone itself.

And did they show you their range of phone covers and screen protectors - perhaps with an enticing 15% off if you buy now offer?

These are all examples of cross-selling.

Cross-selling is simply taking related products and/or services and bundling them into a package in order to get customers to increase their spending.

It's a common practice, but vendors often lose sight of the whole customer buying experience.

Customers will only become advocates if they believe you are offering them great service as well as a great product.

If your new product or service fits well with cross-selling, make sure that it is something useful and valuable for the customer and not just an add-on used to increase sales.

If the customer discovers later that those extra products or services were not worth it, they won't return to buy from you.

What's worse, they may tell their friends, leave bad reviews or even leave negative feedback on social media.

Accessories and Services Supporting the Main Product

In contrast to active cross-selling, accessories and services sell really well but in a more subtle way.

There are whole companies dedicated to selling car furniture, fashion accessories, etc.

Aside from existing cross-selling opportunities, consider whether you can create your own high margin products and services related to your main BIG idea product or service.

Accessories and services don't need much persuasion to sell and enhance the buying experience, provided they are not sold aggressively - rather they are 'discovered' by the customer as part of the buying experience.

For example, Xbox purchasers will probably buy one or two games along with their purchase.

Someone buying a winter coat may well choose to pick out a coordinating hat, scarf and gloves to go with it.

It's always a great idea to try to develop these products and services and, because there is minimal extra selling involved, they often generate higher profit margins and make the buying experience memorable for the customer in all the right ways.

Decide whether to move forward to the
next step with your proposed idea.

If not, pick a new one from your ideas
in the first activity and go through
the assessment process again.

STEP 4

Determine Your

Competitive Potential

If your product or service has little to no competitive potential, it will be just like all the rest in your market.

In this last step of the process, you'll determine if you can provide something unique enough to differentiate you from competitors and build a solid base of sales.

REMEMBER:

Put on your CUSTOMER FOCUS – What will THEY value?

You might surprise yourself!

Activity 9

Congratulations! You are almost there and your **Next BIG Idea** looks like a potential winner.

Right now though, you need to put yourself in the shoes of your customer and really try to think about your new product or service from THEIR perspective while you answer the questions on the next few pages.

Even better, before you fill in your list, photocopy the blank sheets and ask some of your best and most trusted customers to fill them in too — they may well come up with some stuff you didn't think of.

Not all of these prompts will apply, but go through the list and keep in mind the question 'How can I make my Next BIG idea...?'

Product / Service Improvement Checklist	
How can I make my Next BIG idea...	
A luxury purchase?	
More affordable?	
Better value?	
Bigger?	
Smaller?	
Reusable?	
Scalable?	
Bulk orderable?	

Your Next Big Idea!

Bundled with something else?	
Travel size?	
Portable?	
Different colours?	
Personalised?	
One-size-fits-all?	
Uni-sex?	
Safer?	
Healthier?	
More convenient?	
More authentic?	
More modern?	
More convenient?	
More niche?	
More exciting?	
Less scary?	
Service included?	
Installation included?	

D.I.Y version?	
Different pack sizes?	
Longer lasting?	
Disposable?	
Hypoallergenic?	
Organic?	
GMO free?	
Better for the environment?	
Microwave safe?	
Dishwasher safe?	
Recyclable?	
Easier to use / access?	
Wi-Fi available?	
Guarantees / warranties?	
Other?	

Can you make it better for...? Not all of these will apply, but go through the list and answer the question 'How can I make it better for...?'	
Men?	
Women?	
Business Owners?	
Parents of small children?	
Young children?	
Babies?	
Teenagers?	
Young couples?	
New parents?	
The elderly?	
The disabled?	
Wheelchair users?	
Medical conditions such as arthritis, diabetes, hearing impaired, etc.	
Professionals?	

Amateurs?	
Hobbyists?	
Groups?	
Buying out of office hours?	
Weekend access?	
Seasonal access?	
Armchair access?	
Non-English speakers?	
One-off purchasers?	
Bulk Purchasers?	
Regular repeating purchasers?	

Armed with your responses to these questions, now re-frame how you will differentiate your product or service as statements of intent.

Remember to include intangibles such as references, reviews, endorsements, certification, accreditation, access, hours, personal service, turn-around times, delivery options, etc.

These things make a huge difference to potential buyers, so make sure you let them know about yours!

I Will Differentiate By...
1.
2.
3.
4.
5.
6.
7.
8.
9.
10.

This is a necessity!

Activity 10

You will find it impossible to compete if you can't stand out from the competition.

If your customers are locally based

Form a Focus Group and explain the Product or Service concept.

To do this, assemble a group of people from your target market to meet for coffee and cake, with the express task of looking at and discussing your product or service amongst themselves.

Record the session on a webcam or phone and analyse it later.

The focus group can form part of the product or service development process from concept to delivery.

Make sure that the group consists of people from your strongest target market. You defined this in Step 1.

If your customers are not based locally

- Ask them to act as a virtual focus group.

You don't have to meet them in person

- Try using a Google Hangout or Skype Group call instead.

If you have no experience with focus groups

You could employ a marketing consulting group that specialises in setting up such groups.

They can help you form the right questions, gather the right people and they can even hold the sessions at their location.

Describe the concept of your product or service to the focus group

Look for how they react when they hear the explanation.

Then, get feedback from the group on what they like and what they would want to see added to the product or service.

Gather Constructive Criticism

Don't ignore constructive criticism.

This is a great use of the group as it can help you to see how prospective customers perceive your product or service.

You might be overlooking something really crucial that could have a huge impact on the viability of your BIG idea.

Don't Get Defensive

Yes, this is your baby, but now is not the time to start getting defensive about your offering.

Remember that the focus group are there to represent your target market, and if they don't understand or find a fault this is EXACTLY what you have asked them to do.

Better to find out now and be able to adjust or re-think your BIG idea before spending thousands launching a flop.

Arrange a second meeting

Thank the group for their time, and ask if they would be willing to meet with you again once you have moved on to your next step.

Look at Competitors and What They're Doing/Offering

You should always monitor what your competition is doing.

You want to know whenever they are planning releases of new products and services or if they are setting up a strategy that you need to find out about.

It's easy to track what your competitors are doing by setting up alerts using Google.

But how can you measure success when a Product or Service hasn't been created yet?

It would be great if you could look into a crystal ball and have it tell you whether your product or service will succeed or not.

If the product or service does not exist, you need to try and find similar products and services that do exist.

A good way to do this is pose as a customer and ask the question on-line, in groups and forums containing members from your strongest target customer base.

For instance:

"I'm looking for something that will.......... Can anyone help?"

This works for products or services - just phrase your question accordingly.

Once you have some leads...

Investigate them! (see previous steps for how to do this)

What Can You Do That Would Give You a Unique Value Proposition?

The best way to come up with a Unique Value Proposition (UVP) is to get to know your customers' problems, wants and needs AND your competitors' tactics and strategies really well.

It is then a matter of matching up what your customers want with what your competitors are NOT giving them.

It can be something as simple as great customer service, home deliveries, out of office hours, a Twitter help line or free video tutorials on YouTube.

It can even just be getting really good at keeping your customers well informed about your products and services, their uses, and what other plans you have in the pipeline.

Your goal is to make customers feel special, (not stalked!) and also as if they are missing out if they choose to buy from another supplier.

Concentrate on the benefits of your products and services and how they can be used to enrich customers' lives.

DON'T BECOME A PUSHY SALES PERSON!

A perfect example of a company that has a strong and clear UVP is Intuit.

Intuit, the makers of software such as Quickbooks, combines the all-important mention of benefits with a word we all like to hear 'simple' in their UVP, 'Simplifying the Business of Life'.

Another way to differentiate yourself is to offer something extra when it comes to customer service.

For example, a pet grooming company who offers to go to customers' homes during early evenings and weekends so the pet (or owner) does not get stressed, is providing a really valuable service that a customer would be willing to pay extra for (no parking fees, no journey time, no taking time off work, no pet battle, no stress).

Activity 11

Develop a Unique Value Proposition

Your Value Proposition is your promise to your customer of value yet to be delivered.

1. Using a competitor's product or service that you feel closely compares to your BIG idea, list any benefits, features, and potential issues you feel it may have.

Product / Service		
Benefits	**Features**	**Possible Issues**

2. Complete the same assessment using your own BIG idea
    product or service and see how the two compare directly.

My BIG Idea		
Benefits	**Features**	**Possible Issues**

3. Now list all the things you can offer customers as part of your BIG idea, emphasising features and benefits that will set you apart from your competition.

   Make sure that your research has indicated that these are things your target market customers actually want!

   You do not need to fill in all 10 - just a few will do!

My BIG Idea

	Features	Customer Benefits
1		
2		
3		
4		
5		
6		
7		
8		
9		
10		

4. Now taking the information you have, write your own Unique Value Proposition statement that answers the question "Why will customers want buy from me and not from my competitors?"

Why will Customers want to Buy from Me and NOT from my Competitors?

Decide whether to move forward to the
next step with your proposed idea.

If not, pick a new one from your ideas
in the first activity and go through
the assessment process again.

CONCLUSION

Review and Action Planning

By now, you should have a clear indication of whether or not to bring your product or service to market.

Let's review what you learned as well as what to do going forward.

A Review of What You Learned

When you break your product or service evaluation into 4 steps, it helps you determine at each step whether to move forward with bringing your product or service to market or not.

Hopefully you have found the process useful, and have not had to retrace your steps too often, but it is so worth it, and every time you re-trace, you are strengthening your BIG idea AND getting closer to discovering a potential winner!

We've summarised the process in this section and also included checklists for each Step so you can ensure that you keep on track.

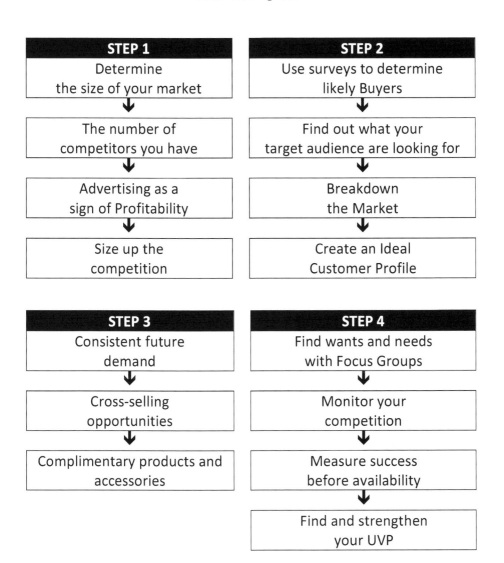

STEP 1
Determine
the size of your market
↓
The number of
competitors you have
↓
Advertising as a
sign of Profitability
↓
Size up the
competition

STEP 2
Use surveys to determine
likely Buyers
↓
Find out what your
target audience are looking for
↓
Breakdown
the Market
↓
Create an Ideal
Customer Profile

STEP 3
Consistent future
demand
↓
Cross-selling
opportunities
↓
Complimentary products and
accessories

STEP 4
Find wants and needs
with Focus Groups
↓
Monitor your
competition
↓
Measure success
before availability
↓
Find and strengthen
your UVP

REMEMBER:

- Customers buy because they have a problem that they want solved.
- Get to know your customers and competitors really well... and keep learning from them.
- A bad product will not sell in the long term, even if the marketing and service are great.
- Repeat customers are a gold mine.
- Don't get complacent - others will try to move into your niche once they see it is working.
- Keep one step ahead.

Tips for Moving Forward

If you have got to this point, and your BIG idea has passed through all the tests, there's a good chance you are now considering bringing your product or service to market.

If the product is a physical one, you will need to either make it yourself, or find a third party manufacturer to handle it for you.

If you are rolling out a service you will need to set the pricing and delivery method in place.

Either way, start with a prototype and do some testing on a small scale with your target market before moving into a full launch.

For funding, if you need it, in addition to approaching your bank, seek out venture capital and crowdfunding opportunities.

You will need to create a business plan and decide how much of your business you are willing to give up in exchange for venture capital investment.

The work you have completed in this book, which shows you have thoroughly investigated and researched your target market, the competition and shown potential sales volumes, will demonstrate to any investor why your BIG idea is worth their backing.

For crowdfunding, you will have to determine what you want to give the people who pledge money to your campaign.

It could be as simple as the product or service itself.

For information products, you can create an excerpt of your product and use that as a giveaway.

To be absolutely certain that your idea will be a success, always test it out with a small segment of your market first – whether current customers or a test group.

You can offer it at an 'introductory' price in exchange for getting honest feedback.

By doing this type of test, you can see whether the idea will sell at all.

You'll also get priceless feedback on changes to make that will maximise initial sales when you launch it to a larger market.

Activity 12

1. Looking at your notes and results from the activities you completed as you went throuh this book, make a final assessment of the potential profitability of your project, product, or service.
2. If your results aren't too promising, brainstorm other ideas and try the activities again with an alternative.
3. Once you've established a product or service you consider to have potential, start planning your next steps, complete with deadlines.

Your Next Big Idea!

Product/Service		
Task	Notes	Deadline

CHECKLIST: Step 1

Evaluate the Market Profitability Potential

- Complete Primary and Secondary Research
- Perform a Google search for your product or service
- Narrow down your search with Google operators
- Draw up a list of competitors
- Track related ads
- Evaluate your competition
- Sign up to newsletters
- Use Google Alerts
- Buy products and services
- Check products being sold
- Check out digital product marketplaces

CHECKLIST: Step 2

Determine Consumer Demand

- Create a survey or poll to find out what people want
- Create a contest to engage potential customers
- Find forums related to your niche
- Help others and develop trust
- Determine the age and gender of your market segments
- Look for competitors' media kits
- Use Google's Keyword Planner to determine search volume
- Try buyer keywords
- Use Amazon search
- Use Facebook Advert Manager as a tool to get a demographic breakdown
- Create an Ideal Customer Profile

CHECKLIST: Step 3

Assess the Long-term Potential

- Ask yourself if people will want to buy your product or service in 5 years
- Consider products or services that fit with cross-selling
- Consider products or services that fit with accessories
- Make sure it's something useful
- Consider supplemental products and services
- Develop supplemental options if the opportunity is there

CHECKLIST: Step 4

Determine Your Competitive Potential

- Complete the statement, "I can differentiate myself by…"
- Use focus groups to determine competitive potential
- Describe your product or service and gauge responses
- Get feedback
- Monitor what your competitor(s) is/are doing
- Evaluate similar existing products to gauge potential
- Develop your Unique Value Proposition (UVP)

You don't need to wait for your product or service to be developed in order to start some buzz about your BIG idea.

Products and services don't sell themselves and, however great your BIG idea is, you are going to need some additional support.

About us

Kim and I are both based in the UK, but Kim spent a number of years in New York working in one of the world's largest cosmetics companies.

In fact, that was one reason for writing this book. Most books on this subject were written for an American audience, and their customers have very different buying habits and triggers from those on our side of the pond.

Kim's extensive commercial, technical and marketing skills were developed in internationally based business-to-business and FMCG environments, mainly in pharmaceuticals, biotech, chemicals, personal care and food – all highly regulated areas.

On her return to the UK, Kim helped businesses in many different areas of operation – from sole traders to large organisations. As you'll have seen in the course of reading this book, she has considerable experience with early stage start-ups, and has driven three loss-making ventures back into profit as well as sustaining their business growth.

In the last few years she has built an enviable reputation as a specialist in online marketing (including social media, websites, ebooks and ezines, and blogs).

My own background – at the start of my career – was as a fully qualified graphic designer, working in London with a first class honours degree in Design Technology and Sociology and a post-graduate Diploma in Marketing. I designed packaging and branding for some major high street names.

As I climbed the corporate ladder my work with these big retailers took me all over the UK, and into France and Germany too. Then, at the age of 31, I decided to start a family, so I retrained and spent 14 happy years teaching Art, Design and Technology.

In August 2014 I launched Teather Creative Design, and in due course collected two more diplomas: in Promoting Goods and Services using Social Media, and in Social Media Advertising and Promotion.

I've really enjoyed my return to the world of business, and I'm happy to have the skills and qualifications to share what I've learned. These days I specialise in grass roots marketing, with a focus on branding and graphic design.

Kim and I have both been working and training in these fields for many years, and decided to launch our series of courses in book form so that anyone could benefit from our knowledge - even if they can't attend one of our face to face courses or workshops.

All our books are available to buy from Amazon.co.uk as well as through a variety of book shops.

Also, as experienced training providers, Kim and I are happy to travel to your place of work or training centre and present any of our courses personally to individuals or groups.

Please refer to

www.teatherandmorrisononline.com

for details of how to book us.

Sammy   **Kim**

Other Books and Courses in this Series:

- ## Marketing for Beginners

  This course covers all the basic grass roots marketing basics that every company, big or small should be using.

- ## Branding

  Your brand is your most important business asset, yet so many businesses fail to grasp its potential.

- ## Graphic Design for Beginners

  Design, like so much else, is governed by rules of thumb which are learn-able and implementable by any business. No artistic ability needed!

- ## Using Inkscape Graphic Design software

  The open access design program is 100% FREE to download and use, and the quality is on a par with Adobe Illustrator, the design industry standard for print and web graphics.
  This course walks you through from first principles, with diagrams, examples and easy to follow instructions to have you producing your own quality graphics for print and web.

- ## SEO for Beginners

  Search Engine Optimisation is so important if you want your website to rank well on Google. Getting to grips with both 'on page' and 'off page' SEO will help you put your marketing in front of your potential customers.

- ## WordPress for Beginners

  Everyone is talking about WordPress and, according to a recent survey, WordPress powers 22.5% of all websites on the internet including some big name brands. This course will teach you how to get the most out of your WordPress site and how to add blog posts, pages and images and make them Google friendly.

- ## List Building and Lead Magnetics

  How are you keeping in touch with your customers? What if you could connect with them whenever you wanted, at the click of a mouse even when you're sleeping? That's what having an email list is all about. This course will take you through the importance of building an email list for your business and the how, what, where, why and when of building your list.

- ## Psychology of Marketing – why people buy

  When you understand how and when your prospects make buying decisions, you're halfway towards converting them to customers. This course will help you create a profile of your "ideal customer " - the person who perfectly fits your business.

- ## Creating Highly Converting Squeeze Pages

  A squeeze page is a critical part of any kind of online marketing. It's a simple page that urges the visitor to give you their email address in return for something valuable you provide, usually for free. Creating good squeeze pages is a skill marketers must master to be successful in building any kind of online business, or to drive traffic to your offline business. This course will take you through the basics of creating squeeze pages, with the goal of getting the highest conversions possible.

- ## Instagram for Business
  Instagram is the fastest growing social media platform at the moment. This course will take you step by step through how to get started on Instagram through the type of content to post and how to build your following.

- ## Social Media for Business
  Everyone thinks they are a social media expert but using social media for yourself is very different to using it for business. This course takes a look at the world of social media and provides you with the information you need to develop a social media strategy for your business so you can make sure you are reaching the right audiences and using your time wisely.

We love hearing from our readers,

and all the above books also run as online

and live face to face courses too

so please do reach out to us

by visiting our website at

www.teatherandmorrisononline.com

or follow us on social media

and see how we can best meet your needs!

18018193R00059

Printed in Great Britain
by Amazon